Original title:
The Magic of Gingerbread Dreams

Copyright © 2024 Creative Arts Management OÜ
All rights reserved.

Author: Rafael Sterling
ISBN HARDBACK: 978-9916-90-870-9
ISBN PAPERBACK: 978-9916-90-871-6

Crumble and Sparkle

In a land where cookies sing,
And the frosting has a fling,
Gingerbread men start to dance,
In their sweet and sprightly prance.

Chocolate rivers flow with glee,
Lollipops grow on every tree,
Marshmallow clouds fluff and sway,
As silly critters come out to play.

A gumdrop prince on a peach parade,
Sips soda from a jellymade,
Pineapple hats bob up and down,
As candy canes twirl in their crown.

In this dream of sugary cheer,
Every giggle spreads the sphere,
To crumble, sparkle, laugh, and shout,
Join the feast, there's fun about!

Sweets of Serenity

In a world where cupcakes fly,
And jellybeans paint the sky,
Who knew sugar could just roam,
With cookie crumbs making it home?

There's a jelly-lake, oh so bright,
With froggy pals in candy light,
With doughnut boats they paddle fast,
Creating mayhem that will last.

Marshmallows tumble, giggle, and roll,
While licorice whips take their toll,
Toffee trees tiptoe with grace,
In this land, no frown can trace.

While lollipop birds chirp a tune,
Bouncing high like balloons in June,
With sweets that bring such silly dreams,
Life's a blast bursting at the seams!

Fantasies in Cookie Crust

In a world where cookies dance,
And sprinkles happily prance.
Sugarplums in a flour dress,
Whisking chaos, oh what a mess!

Ginger folks with gingerbread smiles,
Running wild for miles and miles.
Candy canes, they twist and twirl,
Creating giggles in a swirl!

Marshmallow clouds float up so high,
While chocolate rivers gently sigh.
Licorice ropes swing from the trees,
Catching giggles on the breeze!

And when the oven sings a tune,
Cookie dreams launch 'round the moon!
With laughter baking, what a scene,
In this land of sweet cuisine!

When Dough Meets Dream

Doughnut holes with silly hats,
Playing tag with sneaky cats.
Cinnamon swirls on roller skates,
Twirl and spin as laughter waits!

The buttercream begins to sway,
As cupcakes join the wild ballet.
Popsicle pals join in the fun,
Popping stories, oh what a run!

Frosted treats and giggling yeast,
Tell tall tales at the snack-time feast.
With every bite, a chuckle grows,
In every crumb, a joke that flows!

When dough meets dreams, the silliness glows,
Sugar sprinkles, oh how it flows!
Dive into this sweet charade,
A recipe for laughter made!

Frosting Fairytales

Once upon a frosting swirl,
Where licorice flowers brightly unfurl.
Gumdrop houses, oh so sweet,
Where gum-chewing gnomes always meet!

Chocolate frogs in silly hats,
Talking tall about their spats.
With jellybean knights on candy steeds,
They fight for fruitcake, oh such deeds!

In frosting fields, the laughter grows,
With marshmallow friends in organized rows.
A whimsical ball spins all night,
In the kingdom of treats, pure delight!

Fairytales baked with a cheeky grin,
In this land, all the sweets can win.
Unleashing giggles, one by one,
In frosting fairytales, oh what fun!

Sleepy Baker's Delight

The baker snoozes, flour all around,
In cookie dreams, he's tightly bound.
Sugar plums dance on his nose,
While pancake fairies put on shows!

With sleepy yawns, he rolls the dough,
And little gingerbreads steal the show.
Chasing shadows of rising bread,
While frosting falls on sleepy head!

Sneaky sprinkles jump in the mix,
For giggling laughter, they are the fix.
In sleepy bliss, the dough won't bake,
Till a gingerbread man starts to quake!

Awake, oh baker, rise and shine,
For dreams of cookies taste just fine!
His sleepy grin grows ever wide,
In this delight, he takes great pride!

Sweet Whispers of Frosted Fantasies

In a world where cookies sigh,
Gumdrop mountains scrape the sky.
Marshmallow clouds begin to cheer,
Lollipop laughter fills the sphere.

Bakers dance in rainbow hats,
Juggling pies and furry cats.
Frosting rivers twist and twirl,
While caramel waves begin to swirl.

Candied creatures prance and play,
Filling jars by the bay.
Chocolate frogs leap with glee,
On a tongue, so luscious, free.

Enchanted Crumbs Beneath the Moon

Underneath the silver light,
Ginger folk twirl in delight.
They toss their hats, oh what a sight!
Crafting sweets all through the night.

With cookie boats they sail away,
Past fudge islands, oh so gay.
S'mores danced like they own the show,
While gummy bears all steal the dough.

Pinecone peaks of candy dream,
With soda springs and whipped cream.
As sprinkles sprinkle the soft ground,
In this joy, no frown is found.

Sugar-Spun Nightfall

As night drapes a sugary veil,
Cupcake clouds begin to sail.
They sprinkle stars like tasty dust,
In baked goods, we place our trust.

Fudge frogs hop from cake to cake,
Eating snacks for goodness' sake.
A donut moon starts to shine wide,
With jellybean stars as our guide.

Whipped cream animals prance and tease,
Tickling noses for giggles with ease.
In this sweet frolic through the sky,
Who would dare ever sigh?

A Bakery of Starry Tales

In a bakery filled with dreams,
Floury wizards conjure beams.
With rolling pins like magic wands,
They craft delights of all sorts and kinds.

Cinnamon fairies sprinkle cheer,
While peppermint pirates sail near.
Every cookie has a tale,
Of adventures in sweet fairy mail.

Brownie lords rule the lands,
Tasting treats from tiny hands.
With chocolate rivers flowing fast,
Their joyous laughter will ever last.

Whirling Confectionery Dreams

In a world where candy twirls,
Marshmallow clouds and licorice swirls,
Gingery giants dance in glee,
Sipping cocoa by the sea.

Chocolate rivers flow so wide,
Peppermint boats in sugary ride,
Lollipop trees sway in the breeze,
Tickling toes with sweet, sweet tease.

Gumdrops rain from skies so blue,
As jellybean birds chirp anew,
Cookies giggle and cupcakes prance,
In this land of a sugar trance.

Then suddenly, a pie takes flight,
With whipped cream wings, oh what a sight!
But hold on tight, don't miss the scheme,
In this world of confectionery dreams.

A Symphony of Spices

Cinnamon can play the flute,
Nutmeg strums a spicy lute,
Ginger claps with frosty cheer,
While allspice twirls and spins near.

The sugar canes all tap their toes,
With candy canes in dazzling rows,
A marzipan jam hits the air,
Taffy joins the dancing flair.

Frosting swirls in sweet ballet,
While jelly gets quite carried away,
Each spice adds laughter to the show,
In a nutty symphony's glow.

Oh, the fun they brew and bake,
Cheesecake dreams that jiggle and shake,
When spices sing, you must believe,
In a tasty jest that won't deceive.

Tales of Sugar and Spice

Once lived a cookie with a grin,
With frosting hair and a jelly skin,
He told the tale of his great escape,
From a hungry kid with a cupcake tape.

A donut rolled to save the day,
On a sugary trail, they both would sway,
With sprinkles flying, oh what a sight,
Sugar and spice took off in flight.

Brownies plotted with a wink,
A fudgey scheme that made you think,
They danced atop the golden pie,
As whipped cream clouds soared up high.

A toast to friends both sweet and round,
In this land where joys abound,
So gather 'round, share laughter and bites,
Of the tales spun on sugary nights.

Enchantment of the Pastry Realm

In a realm where pastries dream,
Eclairs float on whipped cream stream,
Scones wear hats of butter glaze,
In this land, the muffins laze.

Tarts with fruit parade with pride,
Croissants glide, they just won't hide,
A cupcake race against the clock,
While brownies play hopscotch on rock.

Cookies chuckle as they bake,
Pies sing songs while fans awake,
Gummy bears lead a joyful march,
Underneath a sugary arch.

Each bite's a giggle, each taste a cheer,
In the pastry realm, there's never fear,
So dance, my friends, take a big leap,
In a land where desserts never sleep.

Dreamscapes in Dough

In a land where cookies dance,
The frosting glimmers, takes a chance.
Ginger folks with sugar coats,
Sipping tea from candy boats.

Marshmallow clouds and jelly beans,
Where gumdrop gardens burst at seams.
Laughter echoes, sprinkles fly,
Even licorice tries to fly!

The silly chef wears a big, red hat,
He'll bake a cake for his lazy cat.
Cookie monsters sing with glee,
And dandelions taste like brie!

So as you drift on sugar streams,
Always cherish those sweet dreams.
For in this land of baked delight,
The fun continues every night!

Wintry Treats and Wishes

Snowflakes swirl, cookies gleam,
Gingerbread men plot their scheme.
With jelly hearts and icing sprigs,
They gather round to dance like pigs.

A licorice path leads to the fair,
Where candy cane poles dance in the air.
Fudge fountains splash in playful play,
While kids laugh, and spirits sway.

The peppermint wind fills the square,
With chocolate cheers but no despair.
A sprinkle fight breaks out near the trees,
Sweet giggles ride the winter breeze.

So grab a slice, and join the fun,
In the world where sweets are on the run.
With bites of joy, and laughter bold,
Each sugary moment never gets old!

The Scent of Celebration

In a kitchen filled with cheer,
Ginger whirls are drawing near.
Flour clouds and cookie dough,
Even the oven starts to glow.

Cupcake towers reaching high,
As plucky flavors start to fly.
With laughter mixed in every bite,
Oh, what a sweet, scrumptious sight!

A trio of tarts sing a tune,
With marshmallow fluff dancing to the moon.
The sizzle of brownies fills the air,
A cakey fiesta beyond compare.

So lift your spoon, and let's all feast,
On each bizarre but tasty beast.
With joyous hearts, let's bake anew,
For each sweet moment is made for you!

Frosty Fragments of Joy

Snowmen made of buttercream,
Rolling down the hills, they gleam.
With chocolate chips for button eyes,
They giggle as they chase the skies.

Candied fruits on candy canes,
Join in on the winter games.
They twirl and spin with jolly cheer,
While desserts cheer loud, "We're all here!"

Pies with whiskers and goofy grins,
Entertain the playful sins.
Cinnamon dreams swirl in delight,
As laughter fills the frosty night.

So come along, don't be shy,
Join the cake parade, oh my!
With each frosted cheer and grin,
We celebrate where fun begins!

Cookies Through Time

In a kitchen where time tends to bend,
Baking cookies, oh what a trend!
The clock strikes twelve, flour goes flying,
Gingerbread men start giggling and crying.

A whisk flies by with a lives of its own,
Jumping around like a dog without a bone.
The oven hums a ridiculous tune,
While gumdrops dance under the big, fat moon.

Sprinkles land in peculiar places,
On cat's tail and between dinosaur faces.
With each bite, you see through the years,
Laughter bubbles, melting your fears.

Each nibble a journey, so silly and sweet,
In this land of cookies, who can compete?
With every crumb, a new story unfolds,
Bold adventures, worth more than gold.

A Night Beneath Candied Stars

Underneath a sky of jellybean bliss,
Candy canes spiral, a truly sweet kiss.
Marshmallow clouds drift, soft and fluffy,
While chocolate rivers glide, oh so puffy.

Gummy bears bounce, giggling out loud,
Congregating near a lollipop crowd.
With each swirl and twirl, folks seem to sway,
Who knew the night could transform this way?

Licorice whips toss a light-hearted game,
As cookie crumbles set the night aflame.
Beneath this sweet sky, all worries unwind,
Laughing till dawn, all troubles left behind.

And as the moon dips in a butter cream glow,
We stash goodies while secrets continue to flow.
In this candied world where dreams intertwine,
Happiness reigns, as we all dine divine.

Sugar-capped Adventures

On a plate so grand, where sweet dreams lie,
Marzipan mountains reach up to the sky.
A jellybean pilot takes to the air,
With cookie-shaped clouds and jellyfish flair.

Each lick of frosting, a tale to be spun,
Chocolate chip pirates yelling, "We're having fun!"
With every sweet step on this sticky terrain,
Laughter erupts, like dancing champagne.

Nuggets of caramel, treasures for all,
We roll and we tumble, with no fear of a fall.
Gumdrops and giggles, in a festival haze,
Beneath frosting rainbows, we spend our days.

So let's venture forth, on this sugar-filled quest,
In a world made of giggles where sweetness is blessed.
With laughter as our compass, and joy as our guide,
We'll conquer this land, with cheer and with pride.

Whimsy on a Platter

Gather round for a feast of delight,
A platter of wonders that sparkles so bright.
With pickles in hats and cupcakes that prance,
Every bite promises a ridiculous chance.

Cheesecake steeds carry laughter galore,
While donuts with sprinkles declare there's much more.
There's whimsy in every savory chunk,
As jellybeans chatter, all grumpy and funk.

Gingerbread critters tell tales of the past,
Of how these absurdities came to be cast.
With cookies as mentors, they counsel the wise,
While licorice lizards teach silly surprise.

So grab a plate and dive into the fun,
In this bizarre banquet, there's room for everyone.
With joy on each fork, and laughter each hour,
Let whimsy unite us, like trickling sour.

Crystallized Wonders of Winter Nights

Snowflakes swirl like sugar doves,
Gathered under stars above.
Cookies dance with sprinkles bright,
Whispering secrets of the night.

Ginger men with frosted glee,
Chasing each other, wild and free.
A peppermint stick turns and spins,
While marshmallow clouds roll and grins.

Whiffs of spice from every side,
Footprints of icing soon collide.
Here in laughter, all feels right,
As snowy tales take wing in flight.

Tales of the Frosted Kingdom

In the kingdom where sweets reside,
The gumdrop mountains stand with pride.
Candy kings in frosted coats,
Ride marshmallow steeds, oh what hoats!

Chocolate rivers flow so sweet,
While jellybeans dance on their feet.
Licorice sticks form bridges wide,
Where sugarplum fairies joyfully glide.

Laughter echoes through the air,
With nutmeg snuggles everywhere.
In every corner, joy takes flight,
In a world that glimmers with delight.

Serendipity in Each Delicious Bite

Nibble here, and take a taste,
Each little morsel, never waste.
Surprises hidden in each layer,
A cookie critter, a crunchy player.

Chomping down on fluffy treats,
The house erupts with happy beats.
With every chew, a giggle sparks,
As candy canes spin silly arcs.

Sweetness sneaks into every grin,
With icing swirls, let the fun begin.
Cookie crumbs underfoot, delight,
In every bite, pure joy ignites.

Memories Baked into Holiday Spirit

Gather 'round the oven's glow,
Flour flies, and laughter flows.
The scent of cookies fills the halls,
As gingerbread men dance 'neath the walls.

Remember when the batter splashed?
We let the racks get sweetly crashed.
A sprinkle here, a smile there,
Baked memories hang in the air.

With each warm bite, the stories grow,
Of shenanigans, and the heat's soft flow.
In this mix of laughter and cheer,
The essence of joy brings us near.

Spiced Enchantment

A cookie army marching bright,
With gumdrop hats and frosting white.
They dance around with sprightly cheer,
While crumbs of laughter fill the air.

A pickle jester steals the show,
With sticky shoes, he steals the dough.
The sugar plum fairy takes a spin,
While licorice twirls her silly kin.

But oh, what's this? A licorice snake,
It slithers by, causing a quake.
The gingerbread knights, all in a row,
Laugh as the licorice swings to and fro.

In this land of sweet delight,
Every bite is quite the sight.
So take a nibble, don't be shy,
In spiced enchantment, dreams will fly.

Tinsel and Tarts

Under the glow of twinkling lights,
Tarts are flipping in cozy sights.
A cupcake elf with a silly grin,
Carves out joy with a grin so thin.

A spatula fights with a rolling pin,
In a kitchen kingdom, let the fun begin.
With frosting naps and sprinkle squalls,
The pastry parade giggles and sprawls.

The grand old pie just won't behave,
It rolls away, a crumbly knave.
Buttercream beasts join in the fray,
As tinsel twirls and sweets play their way.

So bring your laugh and wear your hat,
Join the tarts in their dance and chat.
In this comedy of sugar and dough,
The jolly mayhem is our joyful show.

Nightfall in the Pastry Land

The moon peeks through a glaze of cream,
In pastry land where giggles teem.
A cupcake comet blares its horn,
While marshmallow clouds start to adorn.

A cookie dragon sneezes sprinkles,
Sending gumdrop soldiers in crinkles.
The frosting fountains spray a laugh,
While we all chase the ginger snap path.

A jellybean moonlit ball begins,
As candy canes twist like violins.
The pie parade rolls, oh what a sight,
While lollipops dance across the night.

So come along, don't be late,
In this land where giggles await.
Under starlight, dreams will soar,
In pastry land, there's always more.

Fantasies Laced with Icing

With dreams so sweet in thickened glaze,
Join the fun in sugary haze.
A lollipop lighthouse beams bright and clear,
Guiding lost candies drawing near.

A donut knight climbs icing hills,
With jellybean horses and chocolate frills.
They joust with tarts in frosting swords,
As laughter echoes, it never boards.

A cupcake queen commands the cheer,
Her crown of sprinkles, wildly dear.
Beneath the stars, the cookies laugh,
At tricks played by the sugar staff.

In these fantasies, please do partake,
With every bite, a giggle we make.
So gather round for the sweetest show,
With icing tales that sparkle and glow.

A Symphony of Spice and Enchantment

In a kitchen where laughter spills,
Spices dance on the windowsills.
Sugar sings a sweet refrain,
As flour twirls in a sugar rain.

Ginger giggles in the bowl,
While nutmeg plays its spicy role.
A cookie chorus fills the air,
With sprinkles jumping everywhere.

Dancing dough on the countertop,
Whiskers whisking, they just won't stop.
Molasses joins in with a glide,
As taste buds anticipate the ride.

When the timer gives a cheer,
Out come cookies, full of cheer.
It's a symphony, oh so bright,
In this kitchen, pure delight.

Frosting Dreams and Festive Schemes

In a realm where frosting flows,
Dreams of sweetness softly glow,
Colors swirl in a sugar spree,
While marshmallows float carefree.

Candy canes in a zany line,
Sprinkled gems, oh how they shine.
Gelatin giggles, wiggling too,
As cupcakes prance in a sugary zoo.

Piping bags with a funny twist,
Each swirl knows it cannot resist.
Whipped cream's having a great debate,
On who will be the silliest plate.

Laughter bubbles like hot fudge streams,
As we create our frosted dreams.
So grab a spoon, don't be shy,
And let the sweetness make you fly.

Fantasy Flavors in Soft Butter Clouds

Butter clouds in a dreamy bowl,
Float around like sweetened souls.
Chocolate whispers secret plans,
While cinnamon spins in sassy fans.

Bakers laugh with floury delight,
As doughnuts prance in morning light.
Creamy frosting takes a leap,
Into a world where snacks can speak.

Marshmallows bounce from tray to tray,
While jelly beans arrange their ballet.
Caramel goes for the ultimate dive,
In a pool of sprinkles, oh so alive!

With every crunch and every bite,
Fantasy flavors take to flight.
This joyful feast is unlike any,
In the buttery clouds, there's always plenty.

The Tapestry of Cookie Daydreams

Once upon a cookie night,
Dreams wove tales of pure delight.
Ovens glow with endeavors bold,
As stories of sweetness unfold.

Doughy knights in armor made,
Scoop up giggles, sweet parade.
Chocolate chips like stars so bright,
Shining down with tasty light.

Cakes and cookies side by side,
Join in laughter with every stride.
Sprouted from the spoons of fate,
A tapestry that won't be late.

So gather 'round this golden event,
With frosting mounts and giggles sent.
Let's crunch and munch, all flavors gleam,
In a world of cookie daydreams.

Starry Nights Topped with Spice

Under a moon made of frosting,
Gumdrops twinkle like stars.
Cookies dance in the moonlight,
As we race gingerbread cars.

Laughter echoes through the night,
With candy canes as our swords.
Betsy swipes my licorice hat,
While we guard our sweet hoards.

Icicle lights shimmer brightly,
Rooftops dusted with sugar.
And every giggle that escapes,
Transforms into sweet cookies' huger.

Yet, watch out for licorice storms,
They're a sticky, twisty mess.
High on sugar, we spin around,
It's a wild candy excess!

Whipped Cream Murmurs of the Heart

Fluffy clouds of cream float by,
Where strawberries rule the sky.
I tell my marshmallow secrets,
As they giggle and reply.

A scoop of ice cream whispers low,
Dreams of sprinkles and high-flying meringue.
In a world where hearts are sweet,
Every cup gets its own bang.

Chocolate streams beneath our feet,
With marshmallow bridges to cross.
We giggle as we slurp it up,
No one cares about the loss!

Yet beware the taffy tornado,
It takes your shoes for a ride.
So hold tight your fondest dreams,
As we bounce on gumdrop tide!

Enchanted Glazes and Merry Morsels

A kingdom of cookies stands tall,
Crowned with sugar and spice.
Every morsel holds a tale,
Of kings and queens made of rice.

We're munching on royal charades,
As gumdrop soldiers salute.
Jellybean jesters dance around,
In frosting boots, oh what a hoot!

Glazes twinkle like magic wands,
Painting smiles on every bite.
Pies perform in splendid halls,
In the glow of sugar delight.

Yet, chews might turn to giggles,
As frosting wigs start to slide.
With crumbs and laughter in the air,
It's a whimsical, tasty ride!

A Carousel of Sweet Delights

Round and round the candy spins,
Choco horses prance in glee.
Tinted with peppermint swirls,
Jumping with jubilee.

Cotton candy clouds above,
Whispering tales of the sweet.
We ride on sprinkles of joy,
With lollipops beneath our feet.

Gingerbread hands wave hello,
As marzipan unicorns smile.
In this sugary spinning world,
We can stay here for a while.

But watch for the jellybean flood,
It might wash us away!
So let's twirl on this carousel,
And savor the sugary play!

Sweet Night Whispers

In a cookie land where giggles roam,
The frosting rivers beckon us home.
Gumdrops dance under moonlit beams,
As we chase down our silly dreams.

The candy clouds are fluffy and bright,
With lollipop trees that tickle at night.
Marshmallow creatures jump and play,
In this sweet realm where we laugh away.

The gingerbread folks wear whimsical hats,
And trade their secrets with silly chats.
A peppermint puppy gives a cheer,
While jellybean butterflies flutter near.

Each crumb is a giggle, each bite a jest,
In this world, you can never rest.
So grab a fork and dig right in,
Let the joyous feast of dreams begin!

Spice-laden Dreams

Cinnamon whispers in the chilly air,
While sugar plums frolic without a care.
Pudding mugs dance on the kitchen shelf,
Making mischief all by themselves.

Nutmeg giggles as it adds its flair,
To gingerbread houses with flair to spare.
They tip their hats in a fine parade,
As the cookie crew starts their escapade.

Flour clouds tumble and twirl with glee,
The oven's warmth sings a buttery spree.
Whiskers of cream and popcorn delight,
In this whimsical, sugary night.

So join the feast, let laughter abound,
With spice-laden dreams that twirl round and round.
A sprinkle of joy on every chin,
Who knew baking was such a win?

Sugar and Snowflakes

Frosted flakes drift like sweet little dreams,
Dancing along in sugary streams.
A snowman made of candy canes,
With a jolly laugh that always remains.

Chocolate-covered marshmallows slide,
On the gingerbread slopes, they joyfully ride.
With gummy bear sleds and licorice ropes,
We race through the snow, fueled by sweets and hopes.

The peppermint wind blows funny and bright,
As cookie snowflakes flutter in flight.
Sugar delights encrust our cheeks,
With happy tears from our laughter peaks.

So come and play in the frosting delight,
Where sugar and snowflakes shimmer at night.
Join the dance of the sweet and the fun,
And seize every moment 'til the dreams are done!

Ginger Magic Awakens

As dawn breaks over the gingerbread town,
The sugar rush wakes and spins me around.
With a whisk in hand and a grin on my face,
I shake up the batter in this fun, silly place.

Molasses rivers run yellow and gold,
As the cookie critters share stories of old.
Baking troubles are banished away,
In this land where giggles and gigabytes play.

Here, gumdrops sing and candies do spins,
With frosting flowers waving their fins.
The cupcakes twirl, and the cookies cheer,
For ginger magic is finally here!

So roll up your sleeves and join in the fight,
To bake up a frenzy filled with delight.
In this wild oven of laughter and cream,
Every hour is a glorious dream!

The Crumble of Winter's Embrace

In a house made of laughter and fluff,
The walls are gumdrops, just a bit tough.
The windows are sprinkles, a sugary glaze,
And teddy bears dance in a candy cane haze.

But winter arrives with a frosty surprise,
The roof starts to melt; oh, what a demise!
We run for the hills, leaving crumbs in our wake,
As ginger men giggle, then break for a cake.

A squirrel in a scarf, so dapper and bright,
Complains that our ginger is just not polite.
He twirls on the lawn, doing flips with a grin,
Chasing shadows of frost that are made out of sin.

So watch out for winter, it's got quite the flair,
With biscuits that crumble and laughter in the air.
Our gingerbread dreams may not be around,
But with a chuckle, we'll dance on the ground.

Whimsy Rides on Sweet Cinnamon Winds

The wind whispers secrets of candy and cheer,
While marshmallows tumble, oh dear, oh dear!
With lollipops twirling up high in the trees,
And pretzel sticks bending with biscuit-like ease.

We skip through a meadow of frosting delight,
Where gummies come frolic, alive in the night.
A cupcake parade, all sprouted in glee,
With icing so bright, it winks back at me.

When licorice lakes and chocolate streams flow,
We surf on the fudge, feeling bubbly below.
A troupe of full cookies, in hats made of cream,
Join in our dancing, it's all quite the scheme!

Down the path of delight, our giggles expand,
With churros as friends, we take a grand stand.
As the cinnamon wind tickles our toes,
We laugh at the sweetness, as the laughter grows.

Doughy Dances in Dreamland

In a realm of delight, where dreams come to bake,
Dough boys with twirls make the floors start to quake.
With whisk-twirling wizards and spatulas keen,
They leap through the air like a fluffy baked dream.

The milk rivers swirl in a frothy ballet,
As the muffins and cookies all join in the fray.
Spinning in circles, they laugh with such zest,
With frosting as crowns, they're all feeling blessed.

A jellybean band plays a jolly sweet tune,
While pastries pirouette under the moon.
Giggling, they sprinkle their magic around,
Creating the most delightful of sounds.

As stars made of sugar rise up in the sky,
The doughy friends leap, oh my, oh my!
In joyful delight, they twirl 'til first light,
Then nap in a cookie, till dreams take their flight.

Sugared Shadows of the Past

Once upon a time, in a land made of pie,
Where shadows of sweets would giggle and sigh.
The candied tales told by grandpas of yore,
Were filled with such flavor, we started to snore.

A jelly baby ghost floats in a swirl of cream,
With a wink and a grin, he joins in the dream.
He whispers of cupcakes that sang in the night,
And cookies that twinkled like stars, oh so bright.

Remember the lollipops spinning in place?
And gummy bear soldiers who won every race?
They raided the fridge with a raucous applause,
Leaving trails of frosting and cheering because!

So let us recall, with a grin and a cheer,
Those sugary moments that brought us all near.
Through laughter and snacks, we wander at last,
In a world that takes flight on sweet shadows cast.

The Sweet Abbey

In a kingdom where cookies roll tight,
Gingers mischief at every sight.
Chewy monks with frosting on their heads,
Singing carols while dancing in beds.

Sugar-coated towers rise high,
Marshmallow clouds float by in the sky.
The nutmeg nuns with sprinkles delight,
Baking giggles in the soft moonlight.

Chocolate chip walls hold secrets untold,
In this abbey where dreams unfold.
With laughter echoing through each hall,
Even the licorice cannot help but fall.

Oh, the bundt cake choir fills the air,
Sing of cheer, fly away, if you dare!
Pies in caps, they offer you a treat,
Join the fun, where sweets never meet defeat!

Sprinkled Dreams

In a land where cookies come alive,
Lollipop trees in colors that thrive.
Gingerbread men dance with a twist,
Sipping syrup; who could resist?

Cupcake clouds rain frosting past,
Jellybean showers are a sweet blast.
Giggling marshmallows hop on the scene,
Bouncing around like a sugary dream.

Waffle warriors puff up their chests,
Armed with pancakes, they take no rest.
They joust with donuts, round and bright,
Who will win in this sticky fight?

Sprinkle stars burst forth with glee,
As the candy cane dolphins swim for tea.
A realm of wonder, where fun is the plan,
Join the parade, the sweet tooth clan!

Holiday Hues and Flavors

In a world where cupcakes wear hats,
And cookies chatter like friendly cats.
Gingerbread lanes are bustling today,
With jelly-filled pies leading the way.

Choco rivers flow with dual tones,
Caramel castles made from sugary cones.
Macaron bridges stretch far and wide,
All the treats come out for a ride.

Sour gummies giggle and play tag,
As cinnamon sticks hang on a rag.
Pudding puddles reflect all the cheer,
Each flavor a story, bringing us near.

In this festive land of flavors so bright,
Jolly good times last all through the night.
With laughter and sweetness, our hearts take flight,
Join the fun in this whimsical delight!

Whimsical Frosting Fables

In the realm of whimsical tales, so sweet,
Frosting rivers flow beneath candy feet.
The gumdrop hills are coated in cheer,
Where marshmallow bunnies bounce without fear.

Lemon drops plot in their best silly hats,
Making plans with the starlight chats.
With zany laughter and frosting leans,
Creating stories from sugary dreams.

Cakeland's got giggles in every bite,
With fruit loops dancing in pure delight.
Muffins with stories that twist and twirl,
Invite you to join as the flavors swirl.

Oh, tales of wonders in layers abound,
With frosting flowers sprouting from ground.
So take a seat in this sugary zone,
And let the whimsical fables be known!

Dreamcatcher Delights

A cookie once danced on a plate,
With frosting so bright it would agitate.
It twirled and it spun, quite proud of its shape,
Till it fell on the floor, escaping its fate.

The marshmallow clouds floated high in the air,
Chasing jellybean stars with a fluffy flair.
The laughter erupted, oh what a scene,
As sprinkles rained down, looking quite obscene!

A gingerbread man tried to do a cartwheel,
But lost his gumdrop and made quite a meal.
He wobbled and giggled, a sight to behold,
With a nutty baked smile, so jolly and bold.

So when you dream of treats with a fun twist,
Remember the joy that you surely can't miss.
For each bite of laughter, each slice of delight,
Can turn even dull nights into whimsical flight.

Celestial Cookies

In a galaxy far, where dough meets the stars,
Cookies are flying in their sweet little cars.
With frosting like comets, and sprinkles for speed,
They zoom through the skies, fulfilling each need.

A chocolate chip asteroid drifted on by,
As a sugar star twinkled with a cheeky eye.
They gathered at twilight for a pastry parade,
Making merry as crumbs danced in the shade.

And while vanilla moonbeams lit up the night,
A peanut butter planet shone ever so bright.
With minty fresh rockets that happily zoomed,
Each nibble of laughter in sweetness resumed.

So reach for a cookie, take a bite out of joy,
Let your taste buds laugh like a bright little boy.
For in this wild world of celestial treats,
The fun never ends, and adventure repeats.

Enchanted Dough Tales

In a forest of flour, where fairies do bake,
A muffin-shaped castle began to awake.
With doors made of candy and windows of cream,
The residents baked with a giggle and gleam.

A brownie brigade marched with nuts as their packs,
While cookie sprites danced in their sweet little slacks.
They cheered for the muffins, the jolly old pies,
As laughter erupted beneath sugar skies.

Oh, the jelly-filled waters ran sweet and warm,
Where scones sang a tune like a charming alarm.
With frosting-lit lanterns, the night was alive,
As pastries joined hands in a sugary hive.

So listen closely to the dough tales of cheer,
For each bite of joy makes your worries disappear.
Within this fine realm, let your spirit delight,
As the world of enchantment spins round and takes flight.

Whispers of Sweet Adventure

A licorice river flowed with glee,
Where candy fish swam, wild and free.
The gingerbread boats floated down with a cheer,
Sailing through dreams filled with frosting and beer!

Cupcake mountains towered, oh so grand,
With icing so thick, it was hard to withstand.
Each climb was so tasty, a sugary quest,
Where every brave bite felt like a fest!

The gummy bear troupe danced near the shore,
While chocolate fountains sang tales of yore.
With sprinkles confetti raining from above,
In a land of enchantment, we found all our love.

So join in the laughter, don't miss out on the fun,
For every sweet venture has just begun.
With whispers of joy in each flavor we find,
The sweetest adventures await in your mind.

Frosted Moonbeams

Moonbeams frolic, sweet and bright,
Topping cakes with sugary light.
Baking giggles, whisking fun,
Sprinkling laughter, one by one.

Doughnuts dance in twinkling skies,
With jelly smiles and candied eyes.
Marshmallow clouds drift without care,
While gumdrop stars blink everywhere.

Frosting rivers, flowing wide,
Chocolate boats on a candy tide.
Cuckoo clocks made of pastry bliss,
Waiting for a sugar-kissed kiss.

Silly sprinkles on a pancake stack,
Wobble like a jellyfish on track.
Every bite brings a chuckle, indeed,
In this land where whimsies lead.

Sugar Dust and Wishes

Whimsical wishes on lollipop sticks,
Sprinkling sugar like magic tricks.
Frothy drinks in colorful mugs,
Fluffy unicorns giving hugs.

Chocolate rain falls from the skies,
Cupcake umbrellas, oh what a surprise!
Jelly bean roads twist and twirl,
In a world where sweets dance and swirl.

Candy corns march in the show,
With licorice laces a-glow.
Confetti clouds fluff up the air,
Each munch a giggle, without a care.

Sipping joy from a gumball stream,
In this place where nothing's as it seems.
Sugar dust shining, dreams unfold,
Laughing 'neath the candy-coated gold.

A Carnival of Treats

A carnival stands, full of delight,
With candy apples, oh what a sight!
Cotton candy elephants float so high,
Tickling noses as they drift by.

Popcorn pirates dance with glee,
Their salty tales as tall as a tree.
Giggling cakes ride on a merry-go-round,
In a world where chuckles abound.

Lemonade rivers, fizzy and bright,
Soaking all in the sugary light.
Donut clowns juggle sprinkles galore,
Every laugh opens a new door.

Sassy caramel swirls at play,
Tickling toes in a snack parade.
Laughter mingles with candy's embrace,
In this carnival, find your happy place.

Ginger Tracks in the Snow

Ginger figures leave footprints sweet,
Dancing across the winter's sheet.
Cookie snowflakes whirl and spin,
Each giggle muffled, where to begin?

Frosty windows, icing detailed,
Gingerfolk, with capes, unveiled.
Marzipan trees line the road,
As laughter wraps like a warm coat.

Nibbled paths through powdered snow,
Where candy canes twist to and fro.
Every bite a joy undressed,
In a kingdom where dreams are blessed.

Chuckle with mugs of hot cocoa fun,
As gingerbread houses gleam in the sun.
A sprinkle of humor in every dish,
In this land of frosty, sweetened bliss.

The Night Bakes Beneath the Stars

Under the moon, the cookies dance,
With frosting swirls, they take a chance.
A gingerbread man, so bold and spry,
Chased by a cat that swiftly flies.

Sprinkles rain like falling stars,
While marshmallows play on candy bars.
Laughter echoes through the night,
As doughnuts bounce in playful flight.

The oven hums a silly tune,
Cookies giggle, a sweet festoon.
Whiskers twitch, and flour flies,
In a world where laughter never dies.

As sunrise nears, they blend and sigh,
A cookie chorus sings goodbye.
But don't you fret, they'll rise again,
In dreams delightful, they're still our friends.

Spicy Reveries

Cinnamon clouds in a world so bright,
Cookies frolic in the soft moonlight.
Ginger twirls with a sugar twist,
Laughing as they find what they missed.

Lollipops march with a sweet parade,
Through cookie lands where candy's made.
Chocolate rivers, oh what a sight,
Floating with joy in the starry night.

The licorice trees sway in delight,
As gummy bears dance with fruity sprite.
Jellybeans hop, oh what a spree,
Making merry with sprightly glee.

As slumber falls, the laughter's loud,
In frosted fields, they're ever proud.
Dreams are seasonings, oh so sweet,
In the land where cookies and giggles meet.

Heavenly Sugar Dreams

Gumdrops slide on icing streams,
While gumdrops play on sugary beams.
Cookies chat about their hopes,
In sweetened dreams, with jelly ropes.

Marzipan ducks waddle and weave,
Silly wishes in the webs they leave.
Eclairs giggle, oh what fun!
Racing beneath the morning sun.

Sweet surprises pop from the oven,
While chocolate bunnies do the lovin'.
With every sprinkle that hits the floor,
These sugary delights keep asking for more.

As the sun peeks over the hill,
A gingerbread party gets its fill.
Hilarity reigns in this cookie land,
Baking bliss with a giggling band.

Sugary Moonlight Serenade

Under the stars, a sweet serenade,
Sprinkled laughter in a cookie parade.
Gingerbread folks with big, silly grins,
Celebrate all as the fun begins.

Fluffy marshmallows do a hop,
With licorice whips, they can't stop.
Fudgy brownies roll on the ground,
While cupcake fairies twirl around.

A sprinkle here and a sprinkle there,
Frosting twirls in the sugar air.
Donuts prove they can really dance,
Shaking their glaze in a daring prance.

As night draws close, the fun won't cease,
In their enchanting sugary peace.
They whisper secrets, share a cheer,
In dreams of sweetness, they persevere.

A Journey Through Sugary Land

In a world where cookies prance,
Gummy bears wear hats by chance.
Lollipops dance in sugar's glow,
While frosting rivers gently flow.

Caramel clouds fill the bright sky,
With sprinkles raining from high.
Marshmallow hills bounce in delight,
As candy critters frolic at night.

Choco-bunnies hop with glee,
Cupcake castles grow by the spree.
A licorice bridge, oh what a sight,
Where jellybeans spark laughter so bright.

Snowy mountains made of cream,
In this land, we laugh and dream.
Every corner spills with delight,
Join the fun, it's pure delight!

Twinkling Treats

Under stars of sugary light,
Brownies giggle, quite a sight.
Candy corn shoots through the air,
While peppermint winds twist with flair.

Chocolate rivers, flowing sweet,
Gingerbread folks dance on their feet.
Fudge fountains, oh what a splash,
Laughter echoes, a joyful crash.

Waffles wave with crispy cheer,
Frosting fairies, always near.
Nuts and fruits in a merry mix,
Tasting joy is a clever trick.

As the sun sets in a swirl,
Jelly tots do a bounce and twirl.
In this land, we'll share our dreams,
With giggles, grins, and silly schemes!

Sweet Nightfall Secrets

When dusk arrives with a sweet kiss,
Cookie critters share a bliss.
Covered in sprinkles, soft and round,
They bounce and play without a sound.

Marshmallow pillows line the floor,
While gumdrop friends knock at the door.
Syrup stars twinkle from above,
In this wonder, we find love.

Cinnamon whispers fill the air,
Chocolate milkdares, we'll not share!
Cupcake bright, oh what surprise,
A frosted cake with laughing eyes.

As night falls, the candies gleam,
We join the fun in our wild dream.
Every giggle, every cheer,
In this night, there's nothing to fear!

The Frosting Enchantment

In glistening frosted fields we play,
With wiggles and giggles all day.
Sugar sprites flit about with flair,
Spreading joy everywhere.

Brownie beasts build a silly fort,
Filled with candy, sweet and short.
While pizza pies do a crazy dance,
Inviting all to take a chance.

Frosting rivers twist and glide,
Painting smiles far and wide.
Every nibble brings delight,
In this world, we'll hold on tight.

When moonlight blankets our sweet land,
The giggling treats give a hand.
Join the fun, oh yes, I say,
In this whimsical, wild display!

Dreaming of a Candy Wonderland

In a land where gumdrops grow,
Lollipops dance in a fun, sweet show.
Marshmallow clouds float on by,
And jellybean rivers shimmer and sigh.

A gumdrop prince rides a licorice boat,
While gingerbread folks sing and gloat.
Candy corn trees wave their bright leaves,
Tickled by sweet autumn eves.

Fudge waterfalls bubble with glee,
Singing a tune to a giddy bee.
Chocolate bunnies hop on parade,
Beneath a sprinkle-glitter cascade.

In this world of whimsical delight,
Every day feels just so right.
So join the fun, don't be shy,
In this candy dream, we'll soar and fly!

The Allure of Nutmeg Whispers

Nutmeg whispers from the spice rack,
Telling tales of a merry snack.
Cookies laughing in a warm embrace,
A sprinkle of sugar, a sugary race.

Oh, how the cinnamon giggles and grins,
As batter stirs, and mischief begins.
A dance of flour, a floury spree,
In a kitchen party for you and me.

Rolling pins twirl in a dizzy dance,
While the oven gives a baking glance.
Pies pop out with a giggling cheer,
As we nibble away without any fear.

Whisking away in a holiday dream,
Finding the joy in each fluffy cream.
Nutmeg whispers lead the way,
To a world where sweets come out to play!

Sugarplum Reveries Under Starlight

Sugarplum fairies twirl on twine,
Under the stars, they sip sweet wine.
Glittering shoes with sprinkles so bright,
Twinkling in the magical night.

Cupcake hats and frosting bows,
Dancing under the moonlight glows.
Marzipan voices singing along,
To a playlist of candy spoon-song.

Whipped cream clouds fluff up the scene,
While peppermint sticks waltz like a dream.
Winds that giggle, breezes that tease,
In our world of sugary ease.

So close your eyes, give it a try,
Make a wish and let your spirits fly.
In this place, laughter never seems to cease,
Sugarplum hearts find eternal peace!

Ginger Sighs in the Twilight Glow

Ginger people lounging in twilight's grace,
Sipping sweet tea in a cozy space.
Cookies narrate their crispy tales,
With chuckles that burst like candy trails.

The aroma of spice hangs in the air,
As marshmallow pillows float without care.
Ginger snaps making cheeky remarks,
While candy canes light up the parks.

Biscotti poets write in crumbs,
Creating sweet riddles with giggling thrums.
Licorice laughter echoes the night,
While frosting rainbows swirl in delight.

In a dreamy scene, where smiles abound,
Every giggle is a joyful sound.
So join the fun, don't let it go,
In this twilight glow, we're all ready to flow!

A Baker's Fantasia

In the oven, cookies dance,
Sugar sprinkles in a trance.
Gumdrops giggle, marshmallows sing,
Flour fairies take to wing.

Rolling pins do pirouettes,
Chocolate chips in ballet sets.
Lemon zest wears a party hat,
Doughnuts twirl, and things go splat!

Whipping cream in clouds of cheer,
Cookies waltz while we all cheer.
Pecan pies start to conga line,
It's a feast, oh so divine!

Licking spoons, we have a ball,
Gingersnap confetti falls.
Every bite's a silly spree,
In this kitchen jubilee!

Sugarplum Slumber

In a dream, the sweets abide,
Candy canes and gumdrops glide.
Chocolate rivers flow with glee,
Join the fun, come dance with me!

Peanut butter cups parade,
Donut holes, a grand charade.
Marshmallow clouds fluff up so light,
Jump on in, it's pure delight!

Licorice ropes swing from the trees,
Lollipops chatter in the breeze.
Every star a candy treat,
In this world, we're all so sweet!

When morning comes, the spell will fade,
But sugar dreams, we'll never trade.
We'll keep laughing, never gloom,
As we bake in our bright room!

Frosted Memories

Frosted cakes on sugar clouds,
Candy characters sing out loud.
Sprinkled stars light up the night,
As whiskers laugh, it feels just right.

Baking bats with chocolate wings,
Join the fun as laughter rings.
Sugar socks in a silly race,
Flour dust upon our face!

Gingerbread men with goofy grins,
Cartwheel round as icing spins.
In this place where soft lights glow,
Every moment is a show!

Underneath the marshmallow moon,
We will dance and eat by noon.
Frosted memories brightly gleam,
Living life inside a dream!

Cinnamon Wishes

Cinnamon rolls in cozy hues,
Tickle toes and warm your snooze.
Peppermint sticks lead the parade,
Sugar sprinkles never fade.

Cupcakes wearing silly hats,
Toast to friends and friendly chats.
In this land of treats galore,
Every friend means more and more!

Churros twist in happy lines,
Marzipan makes up silly rhymes.
Taffy pulls like joyful spring,
Laughter is the sweetest thing!

Frosted dreams are here to stay,
Where we dance and laugh all day.
Cinnamon wishes do come true,
In this world made just for you!

Dreams in Icing Lullabies

A gingerbread house with a candy roof,
Where gumdrops giggle and giggles go poof.
Chocolate rivers flow with a bubbly sound,
In a sweet little world where joy is found.

Marshmallow clouds float in a soft, fluffy sky,
Sugarplum fairies do cartwheels nearby.
Licorice trees sway with a whimsical dance,
In this sugary realm, all things have a chance.

Sprinkles rain down like confetti of cheer,
Fudge fountains bubble, oh what a sphere!
Lollipops twirl and swirl all around,
In crispy dreams, happiness is crowned.

Each bite is a giggle, each crumb a delight,
In a land made of sweets, everything feels right.
So close your eyes tight and let laughter soar,
In icing lullabies, we'll dream forevermore.

Cookie Crust Castle

In a castle of cookies, the walls are so sweet,
With chocolate chip guards that can't be beat.
They nod and they wink, and they offer you snacks,
While caramel dragons fly in sugar tracks.

The moat is a pool of warm hot cocoa,
Where marshmallow boats drift, oh so slow.
Gumdrops line pathways, vibrant and bright,
Guiding all visitors with pure delight.

Inside the grand hall, the laughter is loud,
With frosting-covered jesters, they dance for the crowd.
Cookies in armor with jellybean shields,
Defenders of joy in this whimsical field.

So come grab a seat on the icing-rich floor,
In this cookie crust castle, you'll always want more.
With every sweet moment, your worries will fade,
In this realm of wonders that sugar has made.

Frosted Mirth

In a land of pure frosted, all giggles abound,
Candy-coated laughter wraps all around.
Sugar smiles dance under the twinkling light,
With jellybean jests filling hearts with delight.

Gingerbread clowns tickle with frosted hands,
While frosted pancakes flip like floating flans.
Pie faces are served with a sprinkles surprise,
Every whimsy twirling under pancake skies.

Frosted mirth bubbles in a gingerbread cup,
Where gumdrops pop and we all lift up.
Raspberry rain dances on licorice streams,
In this land of sweets, nothing's as it seems.

So laughter runs riot, and joy shares a seat,
In frosted mirth's embrace, life can't be beat.
We'll sip on our giggles and dream 'til we fall,
In this playful kingdom, there's magic for all.

Sweets Under the Moon

Under the moon, where the candies all play,
Chocolate critters dance at the end of the day.
Popcorn clouds drift, all buttery and light,
Landing on gumdrops, a sweetened delight.

Licorice vines twist around lollipop trees,
Soft whispers of sugar float gently with ease.
The moon beams down, like frosting on cake,
While cookies giggle and shake for our sake.

Fizzy drinks bubble, they tickle your nose,
As candy canes rustle in delicate rows.
Marshmallow mice prance on the chocolate chips,
While laughter erupts from the sweetest of lips.

So dance with the sweets, give a wink to the night,
In this land of delights, everything feels right.
Beneath the bright moon, our dreams are aglow,
In a world made of sweets, where fun's all we know.

Cookie Cottage Whispers

In a house made of sweets, oh so neat,
The walls giggle softly, it's quite a feat.
Gumdrops play peek-a-boo in the night,
While licorice laces dance with delight.

The gingerbread folks sulk in the sun,
Wishing their frosting was just a bit fun.
They play hide and seek with the spice jar,
And tell silly tales of a chocolate bar.

The marshmallow clouds begin to rain gum,
While jellybean critters all start to hum.
A cookie cat comes, with a sugar-made hat,
And giggles ensue as they all chat.

As dawn draws near, they prepare for a race,
In a gumdrop car they'll zoom with grace.
With a sprinkle of luck, they'll win the day,
In a world sweet and silly, hip-hip hooray!

Crumbs of Winter's Tale

A frosted forest with cookie tree trunks,
Where marshmallows tiptoe and make silly clunks.
The gingerbread squirrels gather their stash,
In the snow made of sugar, they madly dash.

With peppermint sticks for fun little swords,
The cocoa critters challenge the lords.
A snowball made tasty, with sprinkles galore,
Tumbles through frosty, inviting the roar.

Giggling away, they munch on their finds,
While licorice vines wrap around their minds.
In this whimsical land, no one feels glum,
Each crumb is a treasure, come taste this fun!

As the moon rises high in the root beer sky,
The cookies all gather, oh my, oh my!
With tales of their adventures, they share with ease,
In a laughter-filled night, the sweetest of tease.

A Paranormal Pastry

In a kitchen where shadows can linger and laugh,
A pie with a face gave the chef quite a gaffe.
He winked at the muffins, they giggled in fright,
As the batter began to levitate in the night.

A ghost made of frosting moans softly and sweet,
While cookies chuckle, all jumbled in heat.
They dance in the air with a skip and a jump,
As the flour ghosts play and the candy bars thump.

With sprinkles like stardust, they twirl and they spin,
The doughnuts do join in, with a cheeky grin.
In this haunted bakery, full of delight,
The paranormal sweets give a marvelous fright!

As morning arrives, the fun disappears,
Yet echoes of laughter still linger for years.
The chef shakes his head, quite puzzled and bemused,
In a world full of pastries, he feels so confused.

Charmed Confections

In a land where the lollipops grow on tall trees,
Chocolate rivers flow, tickling your knees.
Marzipan birds chirp the songs of the day,
While the cupcake clouds float gently away.

Candy canes march to their own jolly beat,
While frosted fajitas have a savory seat.
Gingerbread wizards mix potions so bold,
To turn gummy worms into treasures of gold.

A rice krispie dragon breathes marshmallow fire,
While toffee trolls softly strum their lyre.
The prancing cupcakes twirl in sweet bliss,
With sprinkles on top, they laugh and they kiss.

In this charming land where desserts come alive,
Funny and tasty, it's quite the surprise.
So come take a tour where the confections play,
In a whimsical world where sweets rule the day!

Cinnamon Wishes in Sugar-Coated Clouds

In a cookie land where sprinkles dance,
Gingerbread men twirl in a jolly prance.
Chocolate rivers flow with sweet delight,
As marshmallow clouds glow soft and bright.

Cinnamon wishes float on a breeze,
While licorice trees sway with such ease.
Frosty the snowman does a little jig,
With a ginger snap hat, he's feeling big.

The gumdrop trails lead to laughter loud,
With candy canes forming a happy crowd.
Sugar plumbs bounce, keeping time with the beat,
In a world where sweets make life so sweet.

So grab a spoon made of peppermint swirl,
Let's dive in the fun, give the batter a twirl.
In this land of dreams, all's sugary bright,
Join the feast of joy, all through the night.

Cookie Castles Under Starlight

In the kingdom of sweets where cookies reside,
A biscuit brigade goes forth with pride.
Marzipan knights in a royal parade,
Their frosting shields bright, never to fade.

Gummy bears guard the gingerbread gate,
While candy corn plays a cheeky fate.
Jellybean dragons soar through the sky,
Shooting sugar rays as they flit by.

With gumdrops for towers, oh what a sight!
Cookie castles gleam under starlight.
Frosting flags wave, calling all friends,
In this sweet domain, the laughter never ends.

Plum trolls dance, wearing icing hats,
Sipping sweet tea with chocolate bats.
Under the moon's soft glimmering sheen,
We feast on the fun in this sugary scene.

When Molasses Meets Moonlight

In a bubbling cauldron of chocolate goo,
Molasses whispers, 'Hey, how do you do?'
With a twirl and a swirl, it makes quite a mess,
Together they giggle, causing sweet excess.

Under the moonlight, gooey and bright,
Sugar sprites dance, oh what a sight!
Cookies jump high with a crispy cheer,
While cupcakes compete in a frosting smear.

Licorice lassos twine round the fun,
As butterscotch suns begin to run.
In a world where calories don't count at all,
Together they play, they party, they sprawl.

When molasses meets moonlight, the laughter runs free,
Join the sweet revel, just you and me.
In this whimsical night, with stories to tell,
Come join us, dear friend, in our sugary spell.

Frosted Fairytales in a Whisk

In a world where cupcakes take flight,
And frosting fairies glow in the night.
Whisking up wonders, they swirl and twirl,
Creating sweet tales that giggle and whirl.

With cherry bomb dreams and jellybean kings,
A kingdom of sweets where laughter springs.
Sprinkled with humor and giggles galore,
Each fairytale told, there's always more.

Lollipop forests with layers of fun,
In a race, the gingerbread men always run.
Here in this land, where all dreams conspire,
Sugar high tales, born in the fire.

So whip up a story in your fanciest bowl,
Mix in some giggles, sprinkle joy whole.
With frosted fairytales spun in a whisk,
Join this sweet journey, it's life's sweetest risk.

The Starry Sugar Path

A trail of sweets under twinkling lights,
With candy canes guarding the frosty nights.
Goblins giggle, chasing their fluffy dreams,
While marshmallow clouds drip in marshmallow streams.

The chocolate river flows with a playful splash,
Gingerbread boats sail—oh, what a mad dash!
Cookies in hats dance a jig on the shore,
Baking in laughter, who could ask for more?

Lollipops twirl, spinning tales high and wide,
Candy bar cars take a wobbly ride.
Under the stars, with their sugary glow,
We dance through the night, as the sweet breezes blow.

Whiskers of frosting, gumdrop confetti,
Sweet-toothed beasts roam, not one calm and petty.
Frolicsome fun, oh what joy to behold,
On this sugar path where the stories unfold!

Gingerbread Hideaways

In a cozy nook where the cinnamon swims,
Gingerbread houses with chocolatey rims.
Under the icing, secrets we keep,
Bouncing with giggles, the cookies leap.

Sprinkles of magic fill up the air,
While jellybean critters scamper without care.
Starlit retreats made of frosting and cheer,
Home to gingerfolk, spreading joy far and near.

Underneath gumball trees, shadowy and sweet,
A party erupts, with sweet bouncy beats.
Caramel whispers in the soft, warm night,
As the cookie band plays till the morning light.

Each corner has echoes of biscuit delight,
Laughter erupts—oh! What a silly sight!
In this land of sweet dreams where we tumble and play,
Gingerbread hideaways brighten our day!

Frosted Echoes of Laughter

When whispers of frosting tickle the air,
Giggles erupt with a sugary flair.
Dance from the oven—what a delightful sound,
As dough meets the pan; joy knows no bound.

Sprinkle rainbows fall from a sky made of cake,
Sharing sweet secrets, oh what a mistake!
Cinnamon giggles, icing on the run,
Life's just a ride on a gingerbread bun.

The taffy tree rustles with stories from past,
Where cookies once laughed, their fun built to last.
Tracing sweet echoes that swirl all around,
In this frosted fiesta, true joy can be found.

Round the marshmallow fire, stories unfold,
Of daring adventures and fetes to be told.
With every sweet chuckle that fills the night's gleam,
Here in the warmth of our frosted dream team!

Sugar Dreams Unveiled

In a land where the cupcakes hold court each day,
A marshmallow king wears a frosting bouquet.
Scones gather round for a chattering spree,
While licorice dancers perform joyfully.

Underneath gumball skies, laughter ignites,
Jellybeans jive beneath twinkling lights.
Cookies in costumes parade through the street,
Every nibble's a giggle, oh isn't life sweet?

Sugarplum fairies wearing tinsel-like hair,
Spin tales of wonder with love and with care.
Carving out wishes on cakes made of dreams,
Where sweetness abounds, or so it seems.

So come take a trip on this sugary ride,
Where every bite brings joy you can't hide.
In a world full of laughter, together we roam,
In this dreamland of sugar we make our home!

A Canvas of Sweet Surrender

In a kitchen where giggles unspool,
Flour flies like snow in a bowl.
I slip on a sprinkle, oh what a sight,
Dancing with dough, under warm, soft light.

Rolling out rainbows, what a delight,
With frosting waves and colors so bright.
A castle of cookies, a bridge of macaroon,
In this land of sweetness, I'll be a tycoon.

Gummy bears guard my sugary lands,
While chocolate rivers slip through my hands.
But watch for the cat, she's got her own dream,
A cookie buffet, or so it would seem!

So let's twist our tummies in floury cheer,
Biting off more than we can ever bear.
In this land of laughter, and sugary glee,
Baking becomes our hilarious spree!

Stars, Spice, and Cookie Dreams

Under twinkling lights, we mix and we stir,
With a pinch of giggles and a dash of purr.
A cookie-shaped rocket, let's take off tonight,
Where dreams are baked and laughter takes flight.

Sprinkled starlight on my chocolate chip crew,
Marshmallow moons with a sugary view.
I caught a dream in my gingerbread trap,
Now I'm scaling the doughnut, a sugary lap!

Piping stars on cookies with a rambling spree,
With icing disasters, oh filled with glee!
What shape will my cookie take next? Who knows?
Maybe a hippo in a tutu that glows!

In this world's northern side, all fun and cheer,
Gumdrops are pilots, and candy is near.
We'll sail through these dreams, everyone shall cheer,
A spaceship of cookies, let's volunteer!

Whispers of Spiced Sugar

A whisper of cinnamon twirls in the air,
As cookies conspire behind the fridge chair.
They giggle and chuckle, with frosting so neat,
Who's the best baker? Oh, what a treat!

I built a tall tower of crispy delight,
But it wobbles and teeters with playful fright.
A gingerbread chef, in a sugary coat,
Waving his whisk like a magical float.

With every soft bite, flavors pop like a song,
Fruitcake joins in, singing all night long.
Spiced cookies are marching, join their parade,
Laughter erupts; friends, they won't fade!

So let's start a frosty confectioner's war,
Who can bake sugar that's hard to outscore?
With giggles and sweets, our hearts intertwine,
Creating a masterpiece that's simply divine!

Enchanted Confections

In a forest of sweets where the lollipops sway,
Chocolate fountains flow, leading us astray.
Lemon drops giggle, as gumdrops explode,
Chasing our tails down the candied road.

A licorice line, oh what a sight,
Bouncing jellybeans in a pure sugar fight.
With mints in our pockets and cherries aglow,
Adventure awaits in the sprinkles below.

Caramel rivers, we're diving right in,
Whipped cream waterfalls; let's begin!
With every bite, let the clouds rain fun,
Together we'll shine, like that sweet tooth sun.

So toss up the frosting, let's make a mess,
In this sweet carnival, life is a jest.
In enchanted delights, we dream and we scheme,
Hand in hand, let's ride on a sugar-filled dream!

Milton Keynes UK
Ingram Content Group UK Ltd.
UKHW021349011224
451618UK00023B/226